WHEN GOD SAYS "NO"

WHEN GOD SAYS "NO"

BY KELLY HALL CUNNINGHAM

Copyright © 2020 by Kelly Hall Cunningham. All rights reserved.

Bible verses taken from these translations:

King James Version (KJV)

King James Version. Public Domain.

New International Version (NIV)

Scripture taken from the HOLY BIBLE, NEW INTERNATIONAL VERSION® NIV® Copyright © 1973, 1978, 1984 by International Bible Society. Used by permission of International Bible Society. All rights reserved worldwide.

NIV and NEW INTERNATIONAL VERSION are trademarks registered in the United States Patent and Trademark Office by International Bible Society.

New King James Version (NKJV)

Scripture taken from the New King James Version Copyright © 1979, 1980, 1982, by Thomas Nelson, Inc. Used by permission. All rights reserved.

Young's Literal Translation (YLT)

Young's Literal Translation. Public Domain.

English Standard Bible (ESV)

Scripture quotations are from The Holy Bible, English Standard Version, copyright © 2001 by Crossway Bibles, a division of Good News Publishers. Used by permission. All rights reserved.

New Living Translation (NLT)

Scripture quotations marked NLT are taken from the *Holy Bible*, New Living Translation, copyright© 1996, 2004. Used by permission of Tyndale House Publishers, Inc., Carol Stream, Illinois 60188. All rights reserved.

Living Bible (TLB)

The Living Bible copyright © 1971 by Tyndale House Foundation. Carol Stream, Illinois 60188. All rights reserved.

Revised Standard Version (RSV)

Revised Standard Version of the Bible, copyright © 1946, 1952, and 1971 the Division of Christian Education of the National Council of Churches of Christ in the United States of America. All rights reserved.

Acknowledgments

To Abba Father in Heaven,

    Thank You for sticking with me through the **J**oy, and the **P**ain, from **Spiritual death to Life** , for Your **G**race and **M**ercy, and Faithfulness. You are true to Your Word! You truly had a plan for my Life!

I Love You So Much!

To My Mother (Ada Hall),

I cannot begin to express the love that I have for you. You are a **VERY STRONG** woman who showed me how to maneuver through joy and pain and still keep a smile on my face. **Your womb is Blessed by God!**

I Love You!

To Prophetess Valerie E. Gates,

Thank you for pushing me into the spiritual realm to birth this book. You saw me at my lowest. You prayed for me late in the midnight hour when I couldn't pray for myself. You called and prayed with me even when you were going through your trials and others. You answered your phone without hesitation. You thought it not robbery to stand by me through the Love of Christ Jesus when I thought that I was standing all by myself.

I Love You!

To My Manager Sharon Waymer,

Thank you for toiling with me and being a friend that saw what God had placed inside of me. Years ago, I watched you and longed for a spiritual mother, and He gave me my heart's desire after being separated He sent you back into my life to work the vision in my life. You are a blessed woman of God and I thank you for being on my side.

I Love You!

To The Girls Club,

Francoise Cannon, Leslie Rivers, Melissa Brinkley, Angela Rozier, Keisha Malone, Tiny Greene, Kima Hudson, Letricia Ogutu and Sarah Li…I Love You. Without you, seeds would not have been planted and I would not be glowing. Girls Trip Forever changed my life. A new me came to life because of such strong individuals that you are and the bond that we all share. Grace and mercy shall follow you all of the days of your life. My True Riders!

**I Love each and every one of you!
To My Rocks,**

My son **(Joshua)** and my daughter **(Jocelyn)** who made me get up every single day and live when I didn't want to. You make me laugh, cry when you are going through and push me to be the best Mommy that I know how to be.

I love you with all of my heart!

A Special Thank you ,

To "C"

The one that showed me what true love was, and how to love. You helped unlock the prison doors in my mind. You woke me up out of my slumber and the sun started to shine! You will forever be loved!

I Love You!

To the ones who collaborated on this book and helped bring the vision alive. I will forever be grateful for your kindness and patience. My cousin, **Jamar Stokely, and Editor Tim/Holly VonWald.**

TO THE WOMEN who are coming after me who need help to get over to the other side of the fence. I am here with God leading to help pull you over. **The Best Is Yet To Come!**

I Love All Of You!

Table of Contents

Introduction 11
Do Tell 15
Who Am I? 27
What's Love 33
Repeat 39
Her Journey is Not Over 53
Preparation For The Grave 57
Withered Hand 71
Settling 75
The Counterfeit Vs the Real Thing 79
The Baby 87
Beware of Wolves in Sheep's Clothing 91
The Dreamer 101
Caught Red Handed 105
Roots 111
You're Going to Keep Going in Circles... 117
Who Had She Been Dealing With? 121
A Dark Secret 127
Spiritual Jail 131
The Stripping 135
The Wedding 139
Conception 143
God Had a Plan 147
Strength 159
Ministering 163
Note to the Reader 165

Introduction

There was something special about Chloe. As a child, she was told by many that she was special to God. She was a child who would talk to herself. She was a girl that would often have candid conversations with God. However, as she grew older and as she maneuvered through life's experiences, she began to wonder if the prophetic words spoken over her life had any impact on the things happening in her life.

Chloe dreamt of being Cinderella... longing to be loved... knowing not just anyone could fill that space. She would have vivid dreams and pray at night for safety, talk to God about her fears, telling Him what she wanted in life. Her mother knew she was a special child. She recognized her as being Intelligent and insightful, therefore she kept her busy in all the activities that would make her happy I.e.: basketball, volleyball, track, and cheerleading.

Because her mother knew this world better than her little girl, she wanted to give her all she could before her interests changed as she aged.

Eventually, Chloe grew up and no longer had those candid conversations with God, and dreams of being Cinderella no longer interested her. Everything positive that had consumed her life no longer existed. We all can relate to boredom. As many people say, "An idle mind is the devil's workshop."

There were several young men who pursued Chloe, but she kept to her plan and would not entertain them. Because Chloe did not really know what true love was, she sometimes fell into lust and her eyes began to wander. She wanted a boyfriend but was not sure she could handle it. She was looking for a certain spark. She felt left out and wanted to be more like some of her girlfriends, who were chasing the boys. They made it look like so much fun.

Because she grew up with two brothers, she knew the type of boys that she was dealing with.

She was the only girl in the family, and she saw how they treated their girlfriends. In the back of her mind, she began to question, "I wonder how would my brothers feel if a guy treated me the same way they treat their girlfriends?" No cares in the world.

Chloe, not wanting to disappoint her mother and father, was also afraid of what they would say and do if they found out about her having a boyfriend. Although Chloe was raised by her stepfather, they were very close. It was as if he was her very own biological father; he was her best friend.

Do Tell

In her stepfather's eyes, Chloe could do no wrong.It was as if they were Siamese twins. When you saw him, you always saw her nearby. When he worked on cars, she was right there with him... grabbing the wrench, screwdriver or other tools. Oftentimes,her stepfather would get up in the early morning and go fishing. Of course this meant if her stepfather was going fishing, Chloe and her little brother would go fishing with him.

It was said that Chloe and her stepfather looked alike. He would often compliment her, allow her to sit on his lap and crawl all over him like she was a monkey at the zoo. She enjoyed their playtime and thought he was the best dad ever.

All of Chloe's true happiness went downhill one cold snowy evening when her mother was at work. As kids, when it was cold, Chloe and her younger brother loved to sleep with their older brother. His big body kept them warm and safe. They trusted him.

On this particular night she laid on the top bunk, while her brothers took the bottom bunk. It was late and everyone was snug and fast asleep. The door opened and the light shined on her face. Chloe's stepfather was at the door.

Chloe dreaded to see her stepfather coming into the room, because she knew he was going to make her go to her own bed. She hated sleeping in her own bed, because she was afraid to sleep alone. He slowly went over and whispered her name.

Of course, Chloe did not answer. She was trying to stay still and pretend she was in a deep sleep. He then took the blankets off of her. She dreaded this, because she knew he was going to carry her in her room and make her stay. But Chloe thought wrong.

This time as he threw back the blankets there was something different churning in the atmosphere. Fear gripped Chloe as she felt her gown being pushed up and felt his fingers go between her thighs. Chloe was unsure what to do. She thought, "Should she yell and scream for her brothers' help. She froze until a still small voice said, "Start moving like you're getting ready to wake up."

Chloe did what the voice told her to do, knowing now it was the Holy Spirit speaking. She did just a subtle movement so she would not startle him. She didn't want her Stepfather to figure out she really had been awake. Again, she did what the "still small voice" told her to do and he immediately pulled her gown down and backed away and closed the door.

The Bible tells us what happened when the prophet Elijah hid in fear of his life from the evil Queen Jezebel.

before the Lord, but the Lord was not in the wind; and after the wind an earthquake, but the Lord was not in the earthquake; 12 and after the earthquake a fire, but the Lord was not in the fire; and after the fire a still small voice).

13 So it was, when Elijah heard it, that he wrapped his face in his mantle and went out and stood in the entrance of the cave. Suddenly a voice came to him, and said, "What are you doing here, **In I Kings 19:11-18, the Bible says:**

11 Then He said, "Go out, and stand on the mountain before the Lord." And behold, the Lord passed by, and a great and strong wind tore into the mountains and broke the rocks in pieces Elijah?" (NKJV)

My understanding of this scripture is that while we are going through the most anguished time in our lives, we should just sit still and listen to that "still small voice". When we do, we will get direction from our Father in Heaven and see the salvation of The Lord.

WAIT! *"What just happened"*? The man who her mother trusted, violated her little girl. He said he loved Chloe, but he betrayed her and her mother whom he had danced, sang, cooked, and traveled with.

Chloe was in shock and didn't know what to do. She could not fall asleep; her mind constantly raced throughout the night wondering if that door would open again. Chloe had school the next day. She had never been touched in that way before. What would everyone think of her?...Would she look different? Chloe, being a child didn't realize, her friends and schoolmates had no idea what had happened to her. There were misleading thoughts going through Chloe's mind. Should she tell or should she keep quiet?

For Chloe, that night lasted longer than any preceding it in her mind. Eventually daylight broke and she and her brothers had to get ready for school. Chloe crept about in her room taking longer to dress so she would not have to look into her stepfather's eyes. He left for work, not saying a word to anyone and she stayed in her room until the front door closed. Chloe heard the sound of the car driving away. She felt ashamed as she ran to the bathroom.

She'd cried all night soaking her pillow with the tears of a child whose world was now stained with abuse. Her eyes were swollen from sobbing all night long. She cried uncontrollably as her older brother entered the bathroom.

"What's going on?" he asked.

"Nothing." Chloe replied.

Chloe's baby brother entered the bathroom, while the older brother was still consoling her. Chloe broke down and told them what had taken place while they were fast asleep. SHE TOLD! SHE TOLD! SHE TOLD! The secret that would have lasted for years, only lasted for a few short hours. She was forced to face a fear that every young, innocent girl or boy being violated in that manner should not have to experience...EVER

Her brother told her in a stern voice, "You have to tell Momma."

"No," Chloe cried.

The older brother remained firm. "If you don't tell, I will". . She knew then she had to tell.

(Dear reader, no matter what is happening in your life and of those around you...YOU HAVE TO TELL.. Even if you have someone to be your advocate, it's YOU that has to be your biggest advocate.)?" Her brothers held her close letting her know it was going to be alright and somehow, she knew it would be.

<u>(If you keep all of your emotions bottled up, then you will eventually explode. It's like shaking a bottle of Coke that has never been opened. We hold in those emotions and we do not deal with whatever is going on within us. Eventually, we react and explode with multiple emotions—anger, laughter, tears, fears, etc.</u>) God's word states in **Proverbs 4:23,** *"Keep thy heart with all diligence; for out of it are the issues of life."* **(KJV)**

Chloe faced not only her worst fear, but also a demonic force that was passed down from generation to generation, not the person, but the spirit within the person. *(This generational curse is stopped through them that are saved, and who are willing to change.*

Most people never think about what the next girl or guy is going through even though we pass them by or speak to them on a daily basis.

We need to show compassion. What might save them is a kind gesture, such as a wave, a nod, a hug, or a compliment.)

Chloe was that person. She had become a statistic. A girl who had it all, but now been tossed into the abyss of depression. Chloe went to school that day and pushed through her normal routine, in spite of what just happened to her. When the bell rang and school was out for the day, Chloe dreaded having to go home and face her mother.

When they arrived home, her brother immediately asked if she was going to tell.

"Yes," Chloe said.

The brother walked her in the room where their mother sat curling her hair as she always did. Chloe's brother looked at her and said, "Momma, Chloe has something to tell you."

Chloe broke down and started to cry, squeezing out the pain that was inside of her.

To Chloe's surprise, her mother's skepticism would require her to tell the story over and over again.

"Were you dreaming?" her mother asked.

"No," Chloe whimpered.

"Were you really awake?" her mother asked.

Chloe muttered, "Yes."

Her Mother still could not believe it. "Are you sure?"

"Yes," Chloe answered.

Chloe felt hurt, because her mother was hurt by what she had just heard.

Her Mother made the call to her stepfather's job. He immediately denied everything. He returned home. There was a discussion behind closed doors where the children could not hear.

Did Chloe's mother believe her? Did her mother want to believe her? Did Chloe's mother wrap her arms around her and console her? Chloe became frustrated from all of the questioning, because she was embarrassed.

Disbelief was in the air. At that very moment Chloe started building a wall of protection that would shield her from the hurt and shame, the denial of her stepfather's unspeakable act, and the disbelief radiating from her mother.

Chloe's mother asked, "Do you want me to call the police?"

"No." Chloe answered.

"Do you want your stepfather to leave?" Her mother asked.

Chloe again said "No." She didn't want to hurt her mother even more.

How could this wounded child be expected to answer these questions? How could she be expected to go before people she did not know, just to tell her story and be embarrassed again? Frustration and guilt was all over her and she did not know what to do or say.

Chloe's mother and stepfather eventually divorced some years later. Chloe's perfect family in her eyes was now a broken family with unresolved issues.

REFLECTIONS

Who Am I?

Chloe was a vivid dreamer. God would often speak to her through her dreams. Because Chloe didn't realize God was speaking to her, she usually didn't give much thought to them.

Chloe experienced hardships and loneliness, just trying to fit in. Chloe could be awkward at times, as most kids are in their teens, trying to figure out who they are and how others view them.

In the Bible, the Lord speaks about being *a "peculiar people"* (1 Peter 2:9). **Being peculiar doesn't mean there is anything wrong with you. It simply means you are different, set apart, because you belong to God our Father in heaven.**

Chloe remembers sitting at her grandparent's kitchen table in her late teens. Her grandfather started a conversation with Chloe that would tickle her grandparents in the end. Her grandfather stated he was over a program at church and wanted her to sing.

Her eyes got wide with a twinkle, because she was one of four in the family who could not hold a tune. Immediately Chloe said, "Yes!"

Her grandfather asked what she could sing, and her favorite song that she blurted out was, "Amazing Grace." As Chloe sang, her grandfather would grin and her grandmother was rubbing her hands along the table setting with a smirk on her face. It was time to hit the high note and Chloe went for it. Her grandfather and grandmother boisterously laughed, because Chloe was into her song, not realizing her grandfather had played a silly trick on her.

Later there was an in-depth conversation. GChloe's grandmother asked her a question about the "Facts of Life" and what came along with it. Most teenagers Chloe's age would have known exactly how to answer this particular question.

Chloe, puzzled over her grandmother's question, was clueless. Her grandmother looked at

Chloe in disbelief and said, "What is wrong with you girl?"

Chloe's grandfather calmly interjected, "Leave her alone; she's just acting her age."

When those words came out of her grandfather's mouth, Chloe knew then he understood her. Her grandfather knew Chloe wasn't promiscuous. He knew Chloe had not lived life like the other young ladies her age. She was simply acting like an ordinary teenage girl. Looking back now, Chloe understood her grandparents' curiosity was simply a test to understand her logic of thinking.

Years later, as her grandfather lay on his deathbed, the family surrounded him in the hospital. He went around the room, one by ozone telling each person something he remembered them.

He was unable to get to every family member in the room, but he eventually pointed to Chloe, shaking his finger and said, "You are going to have to watch her."

What was he saying?

At the time Chloe could not understand.

It was years down the road before Chloe understood her grandfather was seeing in the Spirit, the hand of God on her life.

In the Bible God **says,** *"I knew you before I formed you in your mother's womb. Before you were born I set you apart and appointed you as my prophet to the nations."* **(Jeremiah 1:5 NLT)**

(Think about this. GOD KNEW YOUR DESTINY BEFORE YOU WERE EVEN BORN.**)**

Chloe's life was training her for her future. God had a plan for her life (Jeremiah 29:11).

I Corinthians 2:9 NKJV
"Eye has not seen, nor ear heard, nor have entered into the heart of man [or woman] the things which God has prepared for those who love Him."

REFLECTIONS

What's Love

All of Chloe's girlfriends had boyfriends. Although she was content being by herself, she figured: "Why can't I have one too?" Chloe eventually started dating her senior year in high school. His name was Charlie.

Chloe allowed Charlie to place her in an awkward situation. Chloe found herself having to constantly sneak out of the house to be with him.

Had Chloe taken the time to get to know Charlie and his character, she would have never entered into a relationship with him.

Chloe became proud. After all, she was certain she was all grown up! She eventually started having sex with Charlie and this sin took a hold of her.

Charlie's mother knew what Chloe and Charlie were doing was wrong, but she thought their puppy love was cute. Charlie's mother would often give Chloe advice when they would have issues. This advice was rarely in her best interest. Being influenced by this bad advice caused Chloe to rebel against her own mother.

Charlie was a cheater, manipulator, as well as an abuser. He was as sly as a fox and slithered like a snake. Because Chloe did not fully understand God's love for her, she settled for someone who didn't know how to love and appreciate her, which ultimately caused her first relationship to go up in smoke.

Chloe pondered why God commanded abstinence from sexual intercourse until marriage. Once you open the door to sexual sin, you lose the perspective of true intimacy becoming one as man and wife.

All of the moral virtue started falling off of Chloe. Pieces of herself were being lost in Charlie's world. It was Chloe's sinful nature **(that is, her flesh)** that yearned for attention, while her spirit hungered for love, guidance, and direction. **1st**

Corinthians 6:18 says, "Flee from sexual immorality" (NIV).

Charlie was a cheater. Sadly, Chloe did not know Charlie had been making his rounds with other women. This happened on numerous occasions.

Because Charlie was thinking only of himself, he was putting Chloe at risk. She could have had an unplanned pregnancy or even contracted a sexually transmitted disease.

God was gracious to her. He did not allow any of those things to happen to her. God's grace and mercy covers us all day long.

Chloe began to see Charlie for who he really was. She knew she wanted a better relationship than this. She had to get away from Charlie because he was leading her down a road of destruction.

Chloe finally used wisdom and moved away from her hometown to start over and complete her education.

Upon returning home and taking charge of her life, she was very selective as to the type of men she allowed into her life.

During Chloe's newfound independence and adventure, she was introduced to a prominent, successful man named Noah, whom she had never encountered before. Chloe was unsure if she should allow him in her space, because she had just come out of a difficult relationship. There was something about this young successful man that drew her in. He always saw in Chloe more than she recognized in herself. He was attracted to her spirit which he genuinely loved. He constantly stayed on her about going to college to better herself.

He exposed Chloe to a life she always wanted and dreamt about when she was younger. He took her to places which made her want more and she started to see herself differently. She started to grow like a flower and everywhere she went her light started to shine. There was a different love that Noah had for her. He always poured positive affirmations in her life and when they went out, he took her to the best. He always complimented her whenever he had the chance and it was not always about physical intimacy. Noah wanted to be around her just because. He stated to Chloe that he had never before met anyone quite like her. Because of his celebrity status, he never knew if the girls he had recently dated were interested in him as a person or what they imagined he could do for them.. The more time they spent together, she started to fall in love and the walls around her came down. They would stay up nights talking about the future and what they wanted in life. They would cuddle, watch movies, and fall asleep in each other's arms. It was truly a love affair to always remember.

Unfortunately, there came some situations which would somehow disturb the connection that they had and Chloe was forced to move away. Noah and Chloe stayed connected in which he would want to travel to see her. But Chloe knew the long-distance relationship would not last, and they had to eventually go their separate ways. They would often speak on the phone just to catch up, but

Chloe, not knowing what she truly had, started to reject him, because she felt in her heart she did not deserve him.

REFLECTIONS

Repeat

Chloe reconnected with an old girl-friend, Mia, and decided to move in with her after moving back. Her friend Mia opened her home with loving arms, but similarly, they both were recovering from bad relationships with the men in their lives.

Chloe was naive with the ways of the world. She and Mia both enjoyed casual drinking, and card games which would last to the wee hours of the night. They never drank so much as to get drunk, but enough to make them feel mature. Many times, Mia would spend nights with her boyfriend, leaving Chloe starving for companionship and missing Noah.

As it happened, Chloe was living in the same town as her ex-boyfriend, Charlie. Because of her desire for companionship and longing to have again what she had with Noah, she was curious about Charlie.

Where was he now?

Chloe found out Charlie already had a child with another woman, but it did not stop her from calling Charlie for them to meet up.

Chloe soon found that reuniting with Charlie came with new challenges and difficulties.

As their relationship rekindled, Chloe made the decision to move into Charlie's family home, which later became a trap for her. In just a few short months, Chloe experienced the heartbreak she had initially fled from.

God's word states in **Proverbs 26:11**, *"As a dog returns to his vomit, so a fool repeats his folly"* **(TLB)**.

Charlie never changed. He had only become more cunning and conniving. He continued to sleep around. Despite Chloe's loving personality, she lacked self-confidence. Although she knew her lifestyle was contrary to her relationship with God, she still longed for love and acceptance from others.

Chloe can recall at the age of 19 going to a church service with her brothers and mother . The call was made for prayer and Chloe entered the line to request her prayer for a blessing. As she stood in the aisle, she immediately changed her request and silently asked God to give her blessings to her family. As she approached the front of the line the pastor laid hands on her and prayed for her, afterwards asking her to move to the side. She did as requested, standing next to the drums. All of a sudden, the drumbeats entered into her spirit causing an effect she had never experienced. The Spirit of The Living God consumed her with a Spiritual awakening and awareness of His Power. She felt as if it was an out-of-body experience. In the Spirit, He started to speak to her saying "Hey, it's Me." Of course, Chloe was surprised to hear a voice speaking directly to her. He repeated Himself and said to her He loved her and that she was His. He told her He would never leave her nor forsake her. He went on to say she would be VERY SUCCESSFUL! Chloe felt the Spirit of God leaving and she started to ask Him questions about her family. He answered them but it was when she was touched by her mother and another woman in the church she could feel the presence of the Lord leaving.

Because of her newfound spiritual awareness, the fight was now on between her and the enemy who desired to keep her bound!

Thankfully, Chloe did not have to face any difficulties alone. Nor do you have to. God's word says, *"Be strong and courageous. Do not be afraid or terrified because of them, for the Lord Your God goes with you; He will never leave you nor forsake you."* **(Deuteronomy 31:6 NIV)**

Charlie's behavior was having a harmful effect on both Chloe's confidence and inner beauty. Chloe started to stress, because Charlie was not faithful.

Chloe was being mentally and physically abused which had an effect both inwardly and outwardly. She wasn't grooming herself as she had before which caused her beautiful hair to fall out. Her attire was not fashionable as before. She appeared to be just another girl being used and abused. Chloe needed something more. She needed God to deliver her from despair and destruction.

God says in His word in **Psalm 139:8,** *"If I ascend up into heaven, thou art there: if I make my bed in hell, behold, thou art there"* **(KJV).**

Sometimes God allows the very thing that is vexing us to make us.

Every morning around 5:00 am, Charlie would get up and get ready for work. On this particular morning after he left for work, there was a coldness in the room. Chloe fell back asleep and started to dream. In her dream, she was lying next to a python snake covered in a manila blanket. The same blanket she and Charlie would lay under. The snake was so big its tail hung off of the bed. It's back was turned away from her and it was fast asleep. The snake finally woke up, slithered out of the bed onto the floor, put its clothes and slithered out of the room.

Chloe woke up in a cold sweat and fearful wondering, *"What in the world am I dreaming?"* She didn't understand.

God was trying to show Chloe she was sleeping with the enemy. Not just any enemy. It was a cunning python snake.

A python is one of the biggest and strongest snakes. It will crush, squeeze, and swallow you whole. It is very sly. It waits and taunts its prey, knowing what the end would be. Slowly it wraps its body around you squeezing the life out of you.

Chloe was dealing with the python spirit. It was so cunning, so strong, so evil.. Eventually, it would try and kill her. This spirit was coming after Chloe. It wanted her dead. Did Chloe listen to what God was revealing to her? No, she had a choice and her choice was to stay with Charlie, who exhibited the nature of the snake.

Chloe felt unworthy of being loved. In her mind she was stuck and couldn't see her way out. She thought abuse and torment would be her way of life. Chloe lived in fear day after day.

Chloe remembered a story her grandmother told her years ago:

A man who found a snake in the woods and the snake was sick, hungry and cold. The man felt sorry for the snake. So, he took it into his home and fed it. The man placed the snake by the warm fire to keep it warm. He loved the snake and nursed it back to health.

The man thought the snake would become a special friend, but one day the snake reared its evil head and bit the man. In shock, the man asked the snake, "Why did you bite me? Did I not bring you into my home, feed you, bathe you, and nurse you back to health?"

The snake answered with a slither, "You knew I was a snake when you brought me into your home. So why are you surprised?!"

Reflecting on the story, Chloe decided on occasions to take trips home to visit with her mother and brothers. She needed to get away and reacquaint herself with the familiar love she could count on.

On one visit, Chloe stayed with her mother. They laid in bed and laughed until they couldn't laugh any longer. They fell asleep and Chloe had a dream. She dreamed she was in this dirt field running for her life. There were many demons chasing her through this dirt field and they were throwing sharp spears at her.

In this dream, Chloe had to get up the hill and over the fence to safety. After climbing over the fence, she went through a nightclub in a mall. There was a man who opened a door to a limousine for her.

There was something about entering the limousine that didn't seem right. But she got inside anyway and then she would end up right back where she started in the dirt field.

This time she heard, "Help! Help!" As she looked down people were asking her to pull them over the fence. She reached back and grabbed their hands. The others continued screaming, "Help!

Help!" They were wounded, filled with desperation and fear. They made it over the fence again and the dream repeated itself.

Once again, Chloe was at the fence. She heard a shriek, **"Helppppppp! Helppppp me!"** Chloe looked down and there was Sidney Poitier reaching for her hand. She grabbed his hand and pulled him up. At that point, she woke up.

Chloe was afraid again. Was God showing her things to come, she wondered. *Please give me a revelation.* She was shaken, because the dream was so intense.

The next night Chloe didn't want to fall asleep, because she didn't want to dream. She was tired and exhausted from the mental anguish she was going through in the dreams.

Lying next to her mother, she felt safe because her mother was at arm's reach.

"Chloe."

Chloe tensed up. She heard someone whisper her name. She looked over at her mother whose eyes were closed as she was fast asleep.

"Chloe."

Again, Chloe turned and looked at her mother, still asleep. *Am I going crazy?* Chloe wondered. Chloe turned her head to attempt to fall asleep.

Again, she heard the voice.

"Chloe."

Chloe was so frightened. This continued a few more times before Chloe realized her mother had been playing a joke on her all along. Knowing now it was all a joke, Chloe began to relax. They both had a big laugh about it, but Chloe still felt uneasy.

Chloe finally fell asleep and started to dream again. This time she was in this huge house and saw a winding staircase. She had no idea where she was. She just knew she had to climb the stairs.

After climbing the staircase, she finally made it to the top where she saw a room. She entered the room and saw a brownish small box on the floor. It had a distinct design on it. It reminded her of the Alabaster Box in the Bible **(Matthew 26:7).**

Chloe bent down on her hands and knees and picked up the box. As she held it in her hands, the box began to unfold. Each side unfolded: one side and then the other. As each side unfolded, a radiant light shined through. The light was so bright it was blinding.

Chloe didn't feel fearful as she saw appearing out of the box a pair of angel wings. As Chloe watched, the angel wings unfolded and a beautiful angel emerged. The angel hovered in the air as Chloe gazed into its eyes.

Its eyes were unique, small, round and black. The angel's body was white as snow. Its light filled the whole room with its countenance. It began to fly around her and went faster and faster as it moved like a streak of lightning, spinning around in circles.

The angel spoke to Chloe, "This is your blessing," as it pierced through her soul. The angel was none other than the Holy Spirit.

Chloe's dreams would somehow show her what God had been revealing to her all along. **Psalm 37:23-25** says, *"The steps of a good man are ordered* *by the Lord: and he delighteth in his way. Though he falls, he shall not be utterly cast down: for the Lord upholdeth him with his hand. I have been young, and now am old; yet have I not seen the righteous forsaken, nor his seed begging bread."* **(KJV)**

Chloe woke up in tears and told her mother about the dreams she had for the past few nights. Her mother always thought her daughter was special and blessed with the favor of God.

As Charlie continued pursuing Chloe, he kept asking Chloe to move out of state with him. After a lot of persuading, he convinced her, but Chloe could not and would not tell her mother.

Chloe did not seem to have learned her lesson, nor did Charlie desire to change.

After moving, the abuse and disrespect became even worse. It became too much for Chloe to handle. One day, on his break, Charlie drove to Chloe's workplace to convince her to come home with him to have intercourse. Chloe said, "No." He then picked up an orange cone off of the ground, throwing it at her, striking her in the face, which left her nose bruised.

"Wait until you get home!" Charlie screamed at her.

Chloe couldn't take it any longer. She had to get out of there *fast*. She ran to her supervisor and explained to her what happened. In support, her co-workers went to her house to retrieve her belongings. Then, they took her to the bus station. Soon Chloe was on the bus headed home, never to return.

Whew! Chloe could finally breathe. A frightening thought ran through her head. *Where am I going to stay? How am I going to face my mother again?* Chloe finally made it back to her hometown where her older brother met her at the station with open arms.

REFLECTIONS

Her Journey is Not Over

This journey Chloe was on was nothing compared to what was getting ready to take place next.

Charlie came back to get Chloe. He said he wanted to see her.

But thank God, Chloe's younger brother was home when Charlie knocked on the door that day. Charlie was coming to take her back and Chloe knew the gate keeper was there to protect her.

The *protection of God is so great! He rains on the just and the unjust (Matthew 5:45). When you've come out of a traumatic relationship, everything can seem so confusing. You have to be healed and set free before you can dive into another relationship. Otherwise, you will discover you are looking for the same type of love. You will repeat the same mistakes if not greater, because you have not taken the time to learn from them.*

Psalm 46:7-11 KJV

"The LORD of hosts is with us; the God of Jacob is our refuge. Selah. Come, behold the works of the LORD, what desolations he hath made in the earth. He maketh wars to cease unto the end of the earth; he breaketh the bow, and cutteth the spear in sunder; he burneth the chariot in the fire. Be still, and know that I am God: I will be exalted among the heathen, I will be exalted in the earth. The LORD of hosts is with us; the God of Jacob is our refuge. Selah.

<u>Our hope lies in God. He sets the captives free. We usually ask God for who we want. Instead, we should ask God for what we really need. It is God who we really need. We will be in anguish until we fall in love with the Master.</u>
<u>When we look to God, He will be our present help. He alone knew you before you knew yourself!)</u>

REFLECTIONS

Preparation For The Grave

Chloe continued to date Charlie. She found a job at a local restaurant. She really enjoyed working there, because she was making decent money. Chloe thought she was finally on a good path.

But Charlie's abuse was impacting Chloe's life. Charlie came to Chloe's apartment after spending time with another woman, angry from whatever didn't go right with him that day. After a heated conversation, he smacked and kicked Chloe. He made her sleep on the floor without so much as a blanket.

Chloe was shattered as she limped on one leg into work the next morning. She knew she was going to lose her job, if she was late and no call, no show. Chloe felt like a used box, broken, tossed and to be smashed by a trash compactor.

Barry, the store manager, had compassion on Chloe, but not enough to let her call out. After all, being short staffed, he really needed coverage for the day.

There was something about Barry that Chloe liked. Barry was a looker and he showered Chloe with attention. He knew how to console Chloe at the time she really needed it.

Chloe knew Barry was off limits. She had to put Barry out of her mind because he was married. But Chloe started to nurse a crush for Barry subconsciously. She had no clue what the consequences would bring.

Proverbs 16:18

Pride goeth before destruction, and an haughty spirit before a fall. **(KJV)**

A familiar spirit was following Chloe. Chloe was suffering from a generational curse. <u>**Many times, the sins our family commit are repeated in their children and their children's children. Often the consequences for those sins are repeated too. This is why it is so important for a person to**</u>

understand what kind of struggles have been going on in his or her family. The generational curse has to stop somewhere. We who live today have to be bold enough to resist temptation.)

Around 9:30 one evening, Chloe's brother's girlfriend came home to let her know Barry was inebriated at the store.

Chloe told her friend she wanted to see this for herself, because he was always professional.

They went to the store and there Barry was sitting at a booth surrounded by beautiful women. He was a very charming man. He always knew when and what to say that would grab your attention. Chloe confidently went over to the table. "Can I please speak to you about something? It's important."

"Certainly," he smiled and cleared the table.

Chloe and Barry chatted for a while. Then Barry asked, "Can I take you out to lunch tomorrow?"

"Yes," Chloe answered.

Chloe was fighting a pointless battle. Over the past few months, she let curiosity take hold of her. Going into the store was leading her to trouble. But Chloe didn't care. She didn't care that she was robbing another woman of her husband. She was self-deceived. She was full of her own pride. At this moment in time, the grave had started to be prepared. Chloe was sowing the wrong seed through her actions.

When Chloe was a child, she would often sit back and study the adults that surrounded her. The 70's era in which they lived was full of life and all about self-expression. However, this expression carries with it consequences that often not only affected their current generation, but generations to follow.

Chloe was tired of being lonely. She wanted someone to comfort her, a man to complete and make her whole again or so she thought.

The next day she put on a cute flowy summer dress that would surely get his attention.

True to his word, Barry picked her up for lunch. Barry was a man who handled his business. He already had a good career with a steady income. He was much older than Chloe.

He definitely had a way with words. Chloe didn't understand many of the fancy words Barry spoke, but she hung off of every one of them.

Being asked out by a man she not only respected but was very much attracted to made Chloe feel special; but this was a different type of special. Chloe felt more like a woman again. Chloe disregarded all the warning signs she previously experienced, because she could not deny needing someone to love her the way she desired.

In the spirit realm Chloe was digging a hole for herself. It wasn't just any hole; it was her grave. Can't you hear the shovel hitting the dirt?

It wasn't long after, Chloe had a dream. She was standing in front of her great grandmother's house. She was worried about her brother who had been undergoing an enormous struggle. The Angel of the Lord appeared to Chloe as before. The Angel was very large and hovered over her.

Chloe asked the Angel, "Is my brother going to go to heaven?"

The Angel stared at her and said, "You will not have a long life." Chloe woke up in shock, remembering the Angel's words. She didn't understand the dream. All she could think of was what she had asked about her brother. How did it end up about her?

This was God's way of warning Chloe to avoid her destructive lifestyle. The Bible says in **Isaiah 55:8** *"For My thoughts are not your thoughts, neither are your ways My ways," saith the Lord"* **(KJV).**

"My ways," saith the Lord. Thank God that this scripture holds true.

If we do not spend time in the Bible developing the mind of Christ, the devil will fool us. He can distort our perspective on things that are true and twist our thinking.)

The next day, Barry took Chloe out to a restaurant of her choice. He was a true gentleman, opening the car door for her, paying all the expenses and treating her like a woman should be treated.

She was smitten by his conversation. In her mind he was brilliant. He paid close attention to her body language, and every word that came out of her mouth. He would even snicker at some of the facial expressions Chloe made when he made statements that intrigued her. He was asking her thought-provoking questions.

Barry was very much attracted to Chloe. After such a long conversation and a lovely lunch, he drove her home, walked her to the front door and asked if he could come back that evening.

With much excitement, "Chloe said, "Yes." Can't you hear the shovel digging?

Of course, Chloe was over the moon and started preparing for his return. The clock ticked slowly. Chloe was getting impatient with the long wait. *He said he'd be back soon.*

The phone rang. It was Barry! Instead of him coming to Chloe's home, he asked that she come over to his place.

"Yes," Chloe answered without hesitation.

Because Chloe didn't have a car, she called a cab.

On the drive to his house, Chloe thought, *"Where is his wife?"* When Chloe arrived, Barry let her know his wife was out of town on business.

Even though it was very late, they talked until the wee hours of the morning. Chloe didn't want to admit that Barry had similar behavior traits as her stepfather. Although her stepfather had abused and abandoned her and the family, she still missed him. In a crazy way, Barry made Chloe feel secure the same way her stepfather did years ago.

Barry asked her, "Would you like to partake in some libation?"

Li-who? What's that? Chloe thought as she immediately answered, "Why, yes. I'd love to!" Chloe didn't want to ask what was libation, because she didn't want to appear immature.

Barry maneuvered his way to the kitchen.

Chloe had no idea what Barry was doing. Barry could have been getting out a whip or a chain for all she knew. The only thing she really knew was whatever Barry wanted, Chloe wanted too.

Barry came back from the kitchen, a cold glass of beer in his hand. Chloe thought *Oh! Libation! Alcohol. That's what this is. Silly me.*

Chloe and Barry sat a while longer talking. Then Chloe excused herself to the restroom. While Barry wasn't looking, Chloe had marked her glass. She was afraid he might drug her drink when she was away. She didn't want him to take advantage of her. When Chloe came back, she noticed the beer was at the same level as she had left it. A sigh of relief filled her. *I can trust him.*

Barry and Chloe made their way to the bedroom.

Chloe knew this room was off limits, because this is where Barry and his wife slept. Her burning desire led her to ignore the obvious.

Chloe gave herself to this man out of pure selfishness. Can't you hear the shovel hit the dirt?

Whenever we yield to our sinful nature, we blatantly disobey God, as Chloe did. We reap life changing and disastrous consequences.)

Eventually, Barry got Chloe another apartment and started building his relationship with her. She would intently listen to him as he told her about his life's journey. She was in love.

Once again that old familiar spirit had come back to visit Chloe. Subconsciously, she felt safe again as she had when she was a little girl.

The way he stood, ate his food, the positions in which he sat, and the charisma he had mimicked her stepfather.

Oh boy! It sounds sickening and it was. On one hand Chloe had a man, but on the other hand she had her **(step)** father back.

Chloe's fantasies and desires were now coming into existence...although not seeing that r, he was molding and shaping her into what he wanted her to be.

Over time Barry started treating Chloe as if she was his property. She developed a dependency upon him, and she accepted his treatment of her.

Chloe turned to alcohol to suppress her feelings. She couldn't bear to tell Barry what she was really feeling. She couldn't risk losing him. Barry was everything to her. So, Chloe silently, again suffered abuse.

Her stepfather's one touch changed Chloe's life forever. She wasn't the same and she was drawing attention from two abusive men she had encountered, seeking love and trying to fill a void.

Not wanting her family to know, she pushed them away, isolating herself from the world.

Barry was her lover, her family and her world. Barry was crafty in the way he would control Chloe. If Chloe wanted to go out, Barry wouldn't simply say, "No."

Instead, he would ask, "Are you really sure you want to do this? Are you sure that going out right now is a good idea?"

If Chloe wanted to go, Barry would say to Chloe, "I was just coming over to see you." He did show up every time. Barry and Chloe acted as if they were already married with no cares in the world. In Chloe's mind, they were perfect for each other.

REFLECTIONS

Withered Hand

One day Chloe's younger brother came for a visit. They reminisced over old times when they were kids. Chloe and her brother walked to the nearby store and then made their way back to her apartment. Chloe was standing by herself in the kitchen when suddenly her hand shriveled up, making it seem as if she were handicapped.

Chloe was terrified, because she had no idea what was wrong with her hand.

Exodus 4:6-7 (NIV)

Then the Lord said, "Put your hand inside your cloak." So Moses put his hand into his cloak, and when he took it out, the skin was leprous—it had become as white as snow.

"Now put it back into your cloak," he said. So Moses put his hand back into his

cloak, and when he took it out, it was restored, like the rest of his flesh.

Eventually, Chloe's hand stretched back out. Thank GOD! Looking back, she didn't realize the warning God was sending her.

Although Chloe's body was now well, her spirit had become crippled. God was showing Chloe what was going on in the spirit realm. God was warning her of upcoming storms and disaster. Can't you hear the shovel digging?

REFLECTIONS

Settling

Chloe sat in her home, and all she could think about was her grandmother's cherry pie. Soon Barry called. "Chloe, is there anything I can get for you?"

"Yes," Chloe answered. "Can you pick up a cherry pie?"

"You got it!" Barry answered before hanging up.

Barry hadn't arrived yet, but in her mind, Chloe was daydreaming already tasting her grandmother's cherry pie. She could remember the texture of the dough, the sweetness and warmth of the cherries, alone. Chloe was ready to pop it in her oven.

When Barry walked in through the door, Chloe at first thought Barry forgot about the pie. Then Barry sat a bag down he had been carrying in his arms. He pulled out a paper-wrapped cherry pie from the convenience store. *WHAT! This is not the same as my grandma's pies.*

Chloe wanted to put a pie in the oven and smell the aroma of the cherry pie in the air.

You see, Chloe's grandmother's pie took time to prepare. In her mind she was going over the recipe. Instead of Chloe getting the best, she received mediocre.

You see, God wants you to have "The Best" and doesn't want you to settle for anything less. God was giving Chloe revelation. She envisioned a homemade pie made with love and the best ingredients, but instead she settled for a single wrapped cherry pie from the convenience store. Please catch this in the spirit.)

Here's another example. As a child, Chloe and her brothers were taught at a young age to complete their chores after changing their school clothes and completing their homework before their mother came home from work. At times, they would watch their mother come home, change her clothes and prepare dinner. The one thing her older brother was good at was cooking buttery popcorn before school. On the other hand, the younger brother was good at frying homemade potatoes.

One day when they were out of school, her younger brother decided to fry some potatoes and asked Chloe if she wanted some. She was hungry! Half-way through the cooking process, Chloe wanted the potatoes, because they looked as though they were thoroughly cooked. Her younger brother told her they were not finished, but Chloe insisted. Her brother obliged and placed her food on a plate. Chloe poured ketchup on her potatoes as her brother looked on. She then took a bite and the look on her face told the whole story. She'd sold herself short. If she had waited at least five more minutes, she would have had the best potatoes. However, she took the shortcut and settled for mediocre, uncooked potatoes.

REFLECTIONS

The Counterfeit vERSUs The Real Thing

What is a counterfeit? The definition of counterfeit is "made in exact imitation of something valuable or important with the intention to deceive or defraud."

Chloe had been working and living her life all the while knowing she had been living contrary to God's Word.

Chloe knew she loved God, but she also loved this Barry. Time after time, Chloe would go to church. She would receive prophetic words regarding her life. That word was warning her Barry was not good for her. Distraught over what was spoken, Chloe sobbed like a baby. She wasn't ready to hear this message.

She was an emotional wreck. She knew Barry was no good for her. After all, he was married, but she loved him.

In her mind, Chloe was rationalizing. *Surely, it could not be too bad to date Barry. Surely, God would forgive her if she asked God for forgiveness in her mind. That's all she had to do, right?*

She assumed that's all she had to do. *Certainly, God will give him to her, if she keeps praying. Besides, Barry deserved a better woman.*

*We all tend to rationalize away our guilty consciences when we are confronted with our sin. So, we keep telling ourselves half-truths so we can continue in our behavio*r.)

Chloe continued her adulterous relationship with Barry. She justified it by saying, "Barry's wife isn't good for him." She tried time and again to get over the prophetic word spoken to her at church. Surely this word had no bearing over what she and Barry felt for each other.

She began working a second job to keep herself busy.

One day a middle-aged lady walked up to Chloe while she was working and stated she was ready to check out. This lady spoke very softly; she was sweet and polite. Her purchase came up to $7.77. The number 777, struck a chord with Chloe. In Genesis, the Bible says, "*God rested on the seventh day.*" It represented God's completed work of creation.

"Oh, that's a good number," the lady continued and began telling Chloe how much God loved her and how special she was to Him. Then she looked at Chloe, "Can I ask you a question? Why do you want a counterfeit when you can have the real thing?"

Chloe's heart dropped again. She knew the lady was talking about her love life.

The lady gave Chloe a business card and told her to quote what was on the card every day. The card stated: "I am Available To You, For Your Plans and Purposes: **Jeremiah 29:11** School, Family, Career and Ministry".

Chloe was overwhelmed with fear, because she knew God was talking to her. *The Grave! The Grave! The Grave!* It's important to understand God wasn't yelling at Chloe because he was mad at her.

Instead God loved her dearly and was trying to get her attention.

God was warning her of the consequences of her sin. He was trying to deliver her out of the enemy's hand. Unfortunately, Chloe was too stubborn to pay attention.

I Samuel 15:23 KJV
"For rebellion is as the sin of witchcraft, and stubbornness is as iniquity and idolatry. Because thou hast rejected the word of the LORD, he hath also rejected thee from being king."

Chloe called Barry and told him about the conversation she had with the lady in the store. Barry dismissed it, saying, "You can't listen to everything people tell you," and so Chloe followed suit and dismissed it as well.

A few weeks later, a man of God approached Barry while he was on a business trip asking him, "Are you married?"

"Yes," Barry replied.

The man of God stated. "You need to turn from your sin."

Barry came from his trip and told Chloe about the encounter he had. Barry and Chloe both knew they were doing wrong, but they stayed together for the sake of love, comfort and connection.

Hebrews 3:8-18 (NIV)

Do not harden your hearts as you did in the rebellion, during the time of testing in the wilderness, where your ancestors tested and tried me, though for forty years they saw what I did. That is why I was angry with that generation; I said, 'Their hearts are always going astray, and they have not known my ways.' So I declared on oath in my anger, 'They shall never enter my rest.'"

See to it, brothers and sisters, that none of you has a sinful, unbelieving heart that turns away from the living God. But encourage one another daily, as long as it is called "Today," so that none of you may be hardened by sin's deceitfulness. We have come to share in Christ, if indeed we hold our original conviction firmly to the very end. As has just been said:

"Today, if you hear his voice, do not harden your hearts as you did in the rebellion."

Who were they who heard and rebelled? Were they not all those Moses led out of Egypt? And with whom was he angry for forty years? Was it not with those who sinned, whose bodies perished in the wilderness? And to whom did God swear that they would never enter his rest if not to those who disobeyed?

And who was God provoked with for forty years? Wasn't it those who turned a deaf ear and ended up corpses in the wilderness? And when he swore that they'd never get where they were going, wasn't he talking to the ones who turned a deaf ear?

REFLECTIONS

The Baby

Their romance continued. Chloe and Barry knew they loved each other. Often, they would go out to dinner and a movie.

Chloe would sometimes go out of town with Barry on his business trips. She was so happy, but she was trying to hide from God.

One night, while she was fast asleep, God spoke to her in a dream. Chloe was in labor. When the baby was delivered, it was a girl. It was the most beautiful baby she had ever seen. She presumed the baby was hungry and turned to Barry whose back was toward her. She called out to him, saying, "We need to feed the baby." Barry never turned around. Chloe began to ask herself, "Why won't he help feed the baby? We need to feed the baby." Chloe looked back down at her beautiful baby girl, realizing she had died within her arms.

Suddenly, Chloe woke up in a panic. Chloe feared the worst. She would become pregnant and God would cause the baby to die. Was this how God was going to punish her?

The dream reminded Chloe of the story of King David and Bathsheba **(2 Samuel 11).** King David sinned against God with Bathsheba. David was smitten by her beauty. He summoned her to his palace and had an adulterous affair with her. She became pregnant and to cover up the affair, David ordered Bathsheba's husband Uriah to the army's frontline in battle to be killed. Uriah died and David married Bathsheba. Therefore, he sinned against God.

A good read! May this story bless and comfort the many people who are hurt by the guilt of this sin. Chloe didn't understand it, but she really didn't want to understand it. She wanted to do what she wanted, not what pleased God.

One day, she was getting ready for Barry to come pick her up for a date. She was so excited. As she was putting her makeup on, she felt the unction to look into the mirror. When she saw her eyes, she gasped for air, not believing what she was seeing.

She saw a reflection into the window to her soul. Her pupils were pitch black. What was it? She was so afraid she quickly looked away.

The dream of her baby dying and her very soul was in the pits of hell. She was physically alive, but her spirit was completely dead. Her dream had come to pass!

Chloe did not enjoy her date night, Instead, she was full of fear. Her grave had been dug!

REFLECTIONS

Beware of Wolves In Sheep's Clothing

Chloe's spirit had been opened up to the dark world—somewhere...she would not wish her own enemy to have to entertain. She was getting ready to go on a deeper spiritual journey she would never forget.

The phrase "Wolf in sheep's clothing," comes from the Bible. In the King James Version of the Bible **Mathew 7:15 reads:** *"Beware of false prophets, which come to you in sheep's clothing, but inwardly they are ravening wolves."*

You have to be careful who you are entertaining. People come disguised as gentle souls. They come pretending to speak for God, but actually they are so vicious that before you even know it, they have you intertwined with evil.

There was an older lady named Susan who befriended Chloe on her job. Susan told Chloe she loved God. Susan did all the right things in the eyes of Chloe. She went to church. She seemed to have a good character. She listened to Chloe's stories about life and her boyfriend.

But Susan only told Chloe the stories Chloe wanted to hear. She told Chloe how sweet Barry was and how much he loved her.

Romans 1:28

And even as they did not like to retain God in their knowledge, God gave them over to a reprobate mind, to do those things which are not convenient; **(KJV)**

Susan's words were contrary to what Chloe had heard spoken of her beforehand. Susan invited Chloe to her church and Chloe was thrilled at the invitation, because Chloe loved going to church. After church, they went to Susan's family's house for dinner.

One of the main courses was lasagna. Even though Susan's family had been very polite towards Chloe, she felt uneasy and skeptical. So, she didn't eat any of the lasagna. She simply wrapped it up and took it back to Susan's place to eat later.

They arrived at Susan's apartment and Chloe was sitting in Susan's kitchen unwrapping her lasagna to eat. Susan had stepped away, when Chloe noticed a long piece of hair in the lasagna. She wrapped the plate back up without taking a bite and told Susan she would finish it when she got home.

Around this time, strange things began to happen. Chloe started seeing heavily in the spirit. When Chloe arrived home, she felt a sense of darkness around her. Amidst feeling the darkness, she would see flashes of light crossing her path. Chloe, without knowing it, had been turned over to a reprobate mind. The Lord was no longer with her. He uncovered her eyes to see what was hovering around her on a daily basis. God had sent a tormenting spirit as he did to Saul.

1 Samuel 16:14 (NIV)

> *Now the Spirit of the LORD had departed from Saul, and an evil spirit from the LORD tormented him.*

The evil spirit was from the Lord allowed by God to harass Saul as judgment for his disobedience. All created things are under God's control. God removed His Spirit from Saul and allowed this evil spirit to torment him. Yes, God gave permission to the dark world to torment him.

By His mercy, God still protected Chloe. Even in her sin, He covered her. In **Hebrews 12:6,** we are told that God chastises (or corrects) those He loves.

Chloe continued to work alongside Susan on a regular basis and she would ask Susan for confirmation about Barry. Every time she did, Susan would tell Chloe what she wanted to hear, not the truth of what God said.

One day Susan took Chloe to her apartment and Susan's aunt was there. Susan asked Chloe, "Do you trust me?"

"Of course I do," was Chloe's reply.

"If I show you something, do you promise not to tell?" Susan asked again.

"Certainly," Chloe responded.

Susan and her aunt took Chloe to her bedroom. There she pulled out a charm.

"Wait a minute," Chloe asked, "What is going on here?"

"Oh, don't worry about it," Susan and her aunt reassured her. "It's just a trinket. It's perfectly harmless."

"Okay," Chloe sighed and let them continue.

Susan explained to Chloe, "Look at the way this trinket was to hang on the string. You simply ask a question. If the trinket swings to the right, it means 'yes.' If the trinket swings to the left, it means, 'no.' If when you ask the question, and the trinket only goes in circles, it means the trinket doesn't know."

Chloe felt really uneasy. She didn't know what she was getting herself into. She realized the charm was part of the dark world and Susan was a practicing witch.

You have to be careful about who you let lead you. As Chloe watched, Susan asked the charm many questions. The charm began to swing. Sometimes it swung to the right for "yes." Sometimes it swung to the left for "no." Sometimes it swung in a circle for "I don't know."

Suddenly Susan stopped.

"Oh my gosh! My boyfriend is home. He doesn't believe in this!" Quickly, Susan put the charm away and left the bedroom to greet him.

A few minutes later, Chloe was walking across the street to her home when she began to hear things. She was now more afraid of what was going on around her.

She began to walk a little faster. *Is someone following me?* she wondered.

The spirit world began to taunt Chloe. Chloe rushed into her apartment and locked the door. There was something eerie in the atmosphere. Chloe was all alone; she was afraid of her own shadow.

At this point, Chloe stopped sleeping in her bedroom. Something evil lurked there. When Barry was not there, she was afraid of being in the room. Chloe started sleeping on the couch in the living room.

Fear gripped her to the point where she wouldn't go to the bathroom at night, but instead would use a plastic cup to relieve her bladder. She replaced the plastic cup each morning without Barry even knowing what she was going through and where she had been sleeping.

What in the world is going on with me? Chloe wondered. *Am I losing my mind?*

One particular night the demons taunted Chloe.

She would hear a bell jingle at her window and footsteps shuffling at her front door. These sounds would repeat.

Where is all this coming from? Chloe felt that the working of witchcraft she experienced at Susan's house opened up the door of her being tormented.

One night the demons tormented Chloe so badly she no longer could stay in her apartment. She ran out of the apartment to call her mother from a pay phone.

"Mom, it's me, Chloe. I need to come home."

"What Chloe?! It's 2 am in the morning. Get back in the house, pray, and go to bed."

"Mom, please," Chloe insisted while she cried on the phone. "I'm scared. I can't stay here tonight."

Her mother said, "Chloe, you wake me up in the middle of the night to tell me a bunch of noises are bothering you?! Go back home where it is safe."

Chloe, crying, hung up the phone. Looking back now her mother knew she had a spiritual gift, but she didn't understand the depth of the gift.

Chloe was alone, afraid, and uncovered in the spirit. Chloe never spoke to Susan again.

1 John 4:1 says
Beloved, believe not every spirit, but try the spirits whether they are of God: because many false prophets are gone out into the world. **(KJV)**

God allowed the association with Susan to dissolve in order to protect Chloe from further torment.

REFLECTIONS

The Dreamer

During the time Chloe spent with Susan, she would experience horrible dreams. She believed if she would have died at that time, her spirit would not have gone to heaven to be with the Lord. Instead, Chloe believed she would have gone straight to hell, because she knew she was being rebellious.

Before Chloe moved to sleep in the living room, she would have vivid dreams. Because of these dreams, Chloe hated falling asleep.

Although Chloe didn't have a bed, she had a nice, soft cushiony topper, air mattress. One night as she was sleeping, she felt the bed go down all at once as if someone was climbing on the bed. In her sleep she began kicking and fighting. As she suddenly awoke, she realized she had been wrestling in her sleep.

Chloe began to have a series of dreams about fierce storms. One of the dreams was about Chloe being in her home when suddenly the front door would swing wide open. Wind and rain rushed in, flooding her home. Chloe had to force herself to get to the front door and the wind and rain would literally throw her back.

Another dream she had was about snakes and darkness. She was given a flower, and the flower began to take the form of the devil. She woke up unsure what was going on with her. This horror was so real to Chloe. She wouldn't want her worst enemy to be tormented like this. Because of the fierceness of these dreams, Chloe started clinging more to Barry. She thought he could protect her.

Chloe could only rationalize these stormy dreams as being her guilty conscience, weighing on her for the adulterous relationship she was having with Barry.

REFLECTIONS

Caught Red Handed

Isaiah 47:3

"Your nakedness will be exposed and your shame uncovered. I will take vengeance; I will spare no one." **(NIV)**

When people sin, they think no one can see them. God sees and knows everything. After a while, God will expose everyone who continues in their sin and won't repent.

The phone rang; it was Barry.

"You need to find another place to live," Barry said."I'll pay for everything and do all the paperwork. I'm ready to move on. I want to be with you."

"Okay," Chloe was overjoyed. She finally won the love of her life! She thought, "Now he'll be with me every night keeping me safe". She immediately went to look for a larger place.

A couple of days had passed and Chloe had been babysitting her adorable three year old nephew. Whenever Chloe left the apartment, she would always lock her door. After a while the lock began to get jammed. Chloe would have to jiggle her key a few times before the lock would turn.

It was a beautiful spring day and Chloe had to do some laundry. A gentle breeze flowed through the apartment from the opened living room window.

Chloe and her nephew walked to the laundromat to wash clothes. After the clothes were done, they began to skip back to the apartment.

Her nephew raced her back to the apartment. There stood a woman knocking on Chloe's neighbor's door.

Seeing the little boy and Chloe come near, the woman turned and called out to her.

"Hey, Chloe, come here."

Instantly, fear seized Chloe, realizing it was Barry's wife.

No, she's found me!

Quickly, Chloe raced to the door. She just happened to turn the lock with just the right strength to open the door on the first try.

Ushering her nephew inside, Chloe barely had enough time to close and lock the door just as his wife was attempting to push it open.

Whew! That was close. Chloe picked up the phone and called her mother.

"Mom, Barry's wife is here. What should I do?"

"Now, Chloe," Mother chided. "This is your mess. Call the police."

While Chloe was talking to her mother, her nephew went to the living room window.

"Hi" his wife said, standing outside the window.

"Go get your mother."

"Okay," the nephew answered, because he didn't know she was referring to Chloe. He stared at her.

She asked him his name and he answered, saying, "Terry."

Immediately the wife's anger flared, thinking Barry had another son with Chloe! Then she called out to Chloe's nephew again. "Terry! Please, I need you to get your mother."

Again, Chloe's nephew said, "Okay."

Chloe ended her conversation with her mother and called Barry.

Telling Barry what was happening, he said, "I know. I know. She called me a few minutes ago."

"But what do I do now, Barry? I'm afraid."

He answered saying, "I will call her and have her meet me at the house. Meanwhile, pack your bags, and I will return to take you to a hotel for the night. By doing so, hopefully, this will keep her from returning to the apartment."

It was pretty ironic that Barry was worried about his wife harassing Chloe, considering all the grief Chloe had put her through. Even if Chloe said, "I'm sorry," a hundred times, that would not be enough to repair the damage she had done.

The Bible says whatever is done in secret will eventually come out to the light. **Luke 8:17 says,**

"*For nothing is secret that shall not be made manifest; neither anything hid, that shall not be known and come abroad."* **(KJV)**

Chloe was now caught red-handed, just like Cain was when he murdered his brother. Only Chloe had murdered a marriage.

Genesis 4:8 YLT
And Cain saith unto Abel his brother, {'Let us go into the field;'} and it cometh to pass in their being in the field, that Cain riseth up against Abel his brother, and slayeth him.

In spite of Chloe's dreadful sin, God's grace and mercy was still strongly upon her. Chloe didn't know what the wife was capable of.

REFLECTIONS

Roots

The very next day, Chloe and Barry pulled a U-Haul up to the old apartment to pack her belongings for the new place.

Even though Chloe had been given warning after warning, she yet again ignored every one of them. The love she had for Barry was rooted so deep. She didn't know how to get out of this relationship if she tried. Their love was like the roots of an elm tree. The roots of the tree go down as deep as the tree stands tall.

The sin had become rooted within their souls. It would take a powerful force to uproot the sin Chloe and Barry were committed to.

<u>When we think about the roots of things, we can think about trees. In order for a tree to successfully mature and reproduce it must have three important components.</u>

<u>First it requires a stable support network or roots.</u>

<u>Secondly, it requires a sturdy reliable trunk which symbolizes integrity. Third, it requires growth. Growth includes not just the tree getting larger, but includes seed bearing fruit it drops along the way.</u>

<u>The fruit we bear in our lives describes the legacy we leave behind for the next generation. We can sow seeds of kindness, but we can also sow seeds of cruelty. Ironically, we seldom see the fruit of the seeds we leave behind us.)</u>

The problem was, Chloe and Barry did not understand this concept. If they had they would have been able to see the destructive fruit as we see happening in Chloe's life.

Chloe felt lost. She was stranded in her own world, not knowing if she was coming or going. Chloe and Barry were so eager to get out of this old apartment and onto the next.

Chloe felt contentment. Finally, she would have someone laying beside her every night. After they packed up the small items in the bedroom, she went to pack up the air mattress. As she pulled off the cushion protector, she noticed the wetness on the mattress. How did the moisture seep through the cushion leaving puddles in the indentations of the mattress?

Had Chloe spilled water on the mattress? No, she didn't. Suddenly, Chloe realized the possibility of where the puddles came from. During her many nights of her tormenting dreams, Chloe had been sweating night after night, fighting through spiritual warfare in her sleep

Who was this person Chloe had become? How did her life change so drastically? She thought she had beaten the odds, but she was in the prison of her sinful nature. Chloe was in deep trouble.

So many people avoid responsibility for their actions, only to realize the consequences would come sooner than later.

Chloe and Barry assumed moving to another apartment would be enough to resolve their issues with his wife. But running now meant they would only have to continue running for the rest of their lives. As the saying goes, "You can run, but you cannot hide."

Barry started a job search in Florida and in no time a position opened up for him there. This was great news!

All Chloe could think about was the beach, the love, the fun, becoming one and finally having a new start at life.

REFLECTIONS

You're Going To Keep Going In Circles Until You Go Straight

Chloe and Barry were excited about their move to Florida. Sure, there was the task of loading up the U-Haul and an 11-hour drive ahead of them, but nothing could compare to the new life they would experience there. Palm trees, warm weather and best of all, no out of pocket expenses. Barry had arranged with his job to cover the first two months of hotel expenses while they found a place to settle. For Chloe, this was going to be a two-month vacation. They laughed and sang most of the way. One of the songs they sang over and over again became a part of Chloe's and Barry's life. The song sung by Luther Vandross was called *"I'd Rather"*.

I'd rather be beside you in a storm,
than safe and warm by myself
I'd rather have hard times together,

than to have it easy apart
I'd rather have the one who holds my heart.

The plan was simple. Get to Florida. Go to the hotel. What could possibly go wrong? They finally found where the hotel was located. They headed straight for it. All of a sudden, the road curved and they went around the curve looking to the left as they passed the hotel. Chloe and Barry wound up on the main road where they had to endure 30 to 45 minutes of rush hour traffic. Chloe and Barry got back on the right road and started back towards the hotel. They went back around the same curve a second time. Again, they wound up in heavy traffic for another 30 to 45 minutes. They went through this process two more times.

Finally, Barry said, "There's a stop sign right there. Let's go straight to see what happens."

Barry drove straight past the stop sign and there sat the hotel to their right. Hmm. In that moment a light bulb went off in Chloe's head. God was using this illustration to speak to her.

"You will keep going in circles until you go straight."

They made it to the hotel, hot, irritated and tired. God had Chloe's attention. Barry and Chloe finally decided to get something to eat. They took some of the items they intended to live off of into the room. They stored the rest.

The next day Barry went off to work. Chloe woke up in paradise. She could sleep late. She could eat whatever she wanted. What more could a girl want? Chloe was loving the fact that she could depend on Barry.

After a few weeks of paradise, Chloe decided to look for a job. She found one that paid very well. They were both working and getting into a regular routine. That is, until one day…

REFLECTIONS

Who Had She Been Dealing With?

Barry was still married and he frequently got calls from his wife. But she was a woman scorned, suffering in another state. She had a boy suffering with her. At the time, she had no clue Barry and Chloe were in Florida.

When Chloe and Barry moved away, she never stopped to think about how this action would impact Barry's wife and innocent child. Chloe had seen her own parents' divorce. It shook the very core of stability in her family's life. Now this boy was going through the very same thing Chloe went through—all because she wanted to be loved. **It's important to know there are always consequences to our actions, whether good or bad.**)

One time, Chloe and Barry were coming back from an outing. Both of them were very tired. They approached the hotel and had just come up to the stop sign where they were supposed to keep straight.

Barry mumbled something. Chloe disagreed with him. Smack! Chloe felt the sting from Barry's hand going across her face. Barry struck so hard, Chloe saw stars.

Chloe was shocked as she tried to get out of the truck. A chilling realization swept over her. Chloe had no family. She had no friends. She had no one. It was just him and her.

Chloe tried to run from him. But Barry grabbed her, pulling her back in the truck. She was scared because he had never treated her this way before.

All this time, Barry had been hiding the abusive side of himself from her. The control was there, but not so much in the physical.

Barry wanted every part of Chloe to submit to him. Chloe was insecure and the abuse would come more frequently. Chloe slipped into a state of depression, but Barry had a way of pulling her out of it. She started to change.

Chloe became submissive. After being smacked they got out of the car. She tried to cover her face so people couldn't see she had been crying. It was dark out. When they made it to their room she turned to Barry and apologized to him. This only fed his ego.

What wrong had she done to Barry to make him take those hands that loved and held her tight smack her the way that he did? She justified it as him being tired, and overworked. She couldn't go back home because she had no place to go. Chloe was tired of starting over. The next day she went to work trying to figure out if she should call someone. Chloe decided to remain quiet. Wait, the woman who told about being sexually abused and stood up for herself in that moment was silent. She loved Barry and was not going to lose him.

She came home to their hotel. Barry told her he had gone and found an apartment for them to live. Not that he was sorry and that he would never hit her again. She was still shaken, but she forgave Barry and he took her to go see this new place.

It was beautiful! The townhouse had a screened-in lanai and backed up to a pond. They could sit back, relax and watch people feed the birds and fish. It broke a lot of the tension. They couldn't wait to move in.

REFLECTIONS

A Dark Secret

There were many bumps and bruises along the way. Barry stripped Chloe of her identity, forcing upon her to become the person he wanted her to be. He would beat her down mentally, all under the pretense of "building her up." Whenever a man treats a woman this way, it always winds up being a disaster.

Barry had total control over her. She would eventually change everything about herself, looking and dressing older than she really was. Her personality changed from her naturally bubbly self. When people came around, they could tell something wasn't right because of the way she would express her thoughts in conversation and actions Silently, Chloe lived in fear of losing Barry and sometimes how he would react in certain situations. She was afraid of making the slightest mistake.

In this rigid, fear-driven relationship, Chloe forgot how to communicate. The way Chloe moved or looked at life was different. They could be driving down the street and Barry would ask questions on why she was looking in another car. She would often be called out of her name.

All Chloe was trying to do was take in the scenery. But she couldn't tell Barry for fear of how it may set him off.

REFLECTIONS

Spiritual Jail

After a while, Chloe couldn't take it any longer. She slipped into a deeper depression. Chloe hated what she had become. She hated the sin that had taken over her. She was trying to find a way to end her suffering.

She could literally see in the spirit where she was inside of her body banging against her flesh trying to get out. She wrestled within herself to the level of panic, feeling claustrophobic. She felt trapped as if she were going to die. She was suffocating.

Chloe wrestled with everything within her until she had no more strength. Suddenly she stopped and sat down within herself as if she was on punishment being sent to a dark room.

She laid on the floor, helpless, and cried. Chloe could not stand herself. She was sad, scared, and alone. Her life seemed as if it had been snuffed out and there was not a thing she could do. She woke up another day in misery. Then another. Then another. On the inside, her soul was in prison and her spirit was dead.

While Chloe felt dead on the inside, many people thought she had it all. After all they were driving new cars, had a really nice home, and they were a good-looking couple. People complimented them regularly, stating: "You look rich!"

But on the inside, Chloe knew they were poor. For Chloe, it was an awakening to find her place in her eternal purpose. They were lacking spiritual awareness. It was the Master, Abba, Father, King of Kings and Lord of Lords. It was Jesus, Jesus, Jesus! His unconditional love for her.

REFLECTIONS

The Stripping

God was not finished with Chloe. She knew what was going on. God had already stripped her and placed her in a cell within herself. Then God stripped them of material wealth. Barry and Chloe lost the house he was granted during his divorce from his wife. One by one their cars got repossessed. They were barely getting by, and now they were living from paycheck to paycheck. God had warned Chloe not to *be unequally yoked.*

2 Corinthians 6:14 KJV
Be ye not unequally yoked together with unbelievers: for what fellowship hath righteousness with unrighteousness? and what communion hath light with darkness?

God had to deal with Chloe not only in the natural, and the spiritual. God dealt with Barry in the natural. What would hurt a man's pride—one who was constantly looking outwardly for approval? It would be to take away from him his very own possessions.

Everything happened so fast. The divorce was final between Barry and his now ex-wife and Chloe felt the sting of the divorce. She had become one with a married man.

The connection was so deep she could tell exactly when Barry's ex-wife was going to call. Every time Barry spoke with his ex-wife, Chloe became extremely jealous. After all, she was no longer Barry's secret.

What was the purpose of his ex-wife's continual contact with him? Why did she still have access to him? Chloe had to be quiet whenever the ex-wife called. Chloe couldn't answer the home phone because it might anger the ex-wife. He showed no respect for Chloe's feelings. Chloe had no voice in the matter. Barry would often make plans about their son without consulting Chloe.

After a while, Chloe noticed the phone would often ring just when it was time for her to go to work. It was the ex-wife on the other end. Chloe was mad daily. So, Barry would wait until Chloe would leave for work to speak to his ex-wife.

Eventually, Chloe's eyes were opened to what was going on. Chloe was Barry's fiancé. How ironic it was that the tables were now turned on her.

REFLECTIONS

The Wedding

The day Chloe had been waiting in heavy anticipation for was here! It was finally her wedding day! Much to her surprise, she was not nervous. Chloe and Barry were trying to make it right by not living in sin. On the way to the church, Barry's truck broke down on the bridge. As she was preparing to get dressed at the church, she had no clue what was going on with Barry. A police officer picked Barry and his groomsmen up and rushed them to the church.

The time had come to walk down the aisle, but now with both brothers on her arm, fear arose inside of her. She saw this man looking at her and she at him. As she finally made it to the altar, she breathed a sigh of relief. All eyes were on them. They said their vows and had their marital kiss. Beautiful! Upon turning around, the minister pronounced Chloe and Barry husband and wife.

At this moment Chloe heard it—the sudden click of a lock in the spirit. Chloe thought, *"What did I just do? Oh, Lord. Not only am I bound, but I am shackled. I'm deeper in the prison cell."* Chloe knew now she couldn't get out of this marriage. She was afraid of what people might say.

On the other hand, Chloe loved Barry. After all, they were the perfect couple. At least everyone thought they were.

She was so uncomfortable on her wedding day. At this point she knew the two of them were not meant to be married.

REFLECTIONS

Conception

It was on their honeymoon that Chloe conceived. A baby, oh boy! They'd always wanted a girl, still, to find out it was a boy made them very happy. He was so easy to carry. Chloe knew in her heart he was going to be the best baby and son in the whole wide world.

Before the baby was born, Chloe knew he was different. She especially became aware of this when she went to the grocery store. Whenever Chloe would get to the meat section, she would just leave everything in the buggy and run out of the store. Suddenly, she became aware. He doesn't like meat!

Every time Chloe got close to raw meat, she would freak out. When the baby was born, he came out a very healthy, beautiful baby boy. He was so beautiful Chloe could hardly believe he was hers!

He cried…and cried…and cried. He cried all night long as Barry walked the floor with him in his arms. Chloe was exhausted. She needed to get some rest. What was going on?

The doctors ran every type of test, finding nothing. The next morning, the doctors confirmed that the baby was simply hungry. No one had fed him. Poor child! The baby was not fed immediately, because Chloe had just come back from having a c-section and was trying to get some sleep while the baby was waiting to be fed.

After getting him home, he would still cry, unless Chloe was holding him. No one but Chloe could hold and comfort him. He never took naps longer than ten minutes. Barry worked all day and night, leaving Chloe home alone with the baby. She was exhausted.

REFLECTIONS

God Had a Plan

One day, Chloe's friend, Mia called. Mia lived in Alabama while Chloe lived in Florida. Mia had been through abuse as well. She shared her stories with Chloe about her husband and how she got to know the Lord.

Mia explained. "I locked myself in a room. It was me, my Bible and the Holy Spirit, she said. God is feeding me from this book. God has been bringing me to life."

Mia continued to tell Chloe about how the enemy would attack her, try to scare her and make things happen in her home, but Mia would press through.

Mia went on to tell Chloe about a woman she had met at church and suggested they call her.

"Okay. Let's call her," Chloe said.

The woman was mysterious. She shared with Mia and Chloe many things about herself. She shared how she had lived a sinful life and she now serves the Lord. The woman was a prophetess.

The prophetess started speaking into both of their lives. She told Chloe and Mia about their current struggles. Mia and Chloe started to become afraid.

How did she know secret things about them? How did she know, day in and day out that Chloe would sit on the couch holding her son on her lap with his face touching hers? She explained it was a representation of God's face against hers.

Chloe and Mia started calling the prophetess every day. Every so often, the prophetess would tell Chloe and Mia deep revelation regarding their individual sin. This happened over the course of a month. Finally, they were hooked. Everyday Chloe and Mia would call hert.

At this point, Chloe began to see spirits manifest in her home. Barry had no clue what was going on. He was seldom at home, absorbed in his work. The truth is, God was speaking to Chloe and

Mia. Chloe was confused. She didn't know what to do.

Finally, the prophetess t was ready to lead her to deliverance. She said, "Chloe, you need to repent."

Chloe was shocked. "What? Me? Repent? I thought I already did that?"

Still, the Lord showed mercy on Chloe's soul. Chloe had committed adultery. She took another woman's husband. Not only had Chloe committed adultery, but she took a father away from his son. All this so Chloe could have the man she craved.

Chloe was guilty of coveting another woman's husband. She sinned against God. He was not pleased with her at all.

I Corinthians 6:18 (KJV)

Flee fornication. Every sin that a man doeth is without the body; but he that committeth fornication sinneth against his own body.

This is why God allowed her spiritual eyes to be opened, to see the spiritual attack coming against her. It was of her own doing.

This day, the prophetess told Chloe she needed to repent. Immediately, Chloe called upon the name of Jesus.

The Prophetess het said, "No, call on Him like you want Him."

"Jesus," Chloe cried.

"Call on Jesus like you want him," the prophet said again. "Call on his name over and over again."

"JESUS. JESUS!" Chloe cried. She cried out for Jesus and asked for forgiveness until rivers of living water began to flow out of her belly.

John 7:38 (KJV)
He that believeth on me, as the scripture hath said, out of his belly shall flow rivers of living water.

Chloe's mouth began to babble. She didn't know it, but her spirit was reborn! The Holy Spirit was speaking through Chloe to the Heavenly Father.

Chloe was scared, but the water started flowing from her. There was a different language flowing from within. She repented. She called on the name of the Lord like she wanted Him. And the Holy Spirit filled her with a newness of life.

Chloe would never be the same. She would talk to the prophetess het daily as she was being led and guided. Looking back, she knew the prophetess was truly from God, speaking to her about destruction and salvation. She spoke directly to Chloe's soul!

Before her newfound salvation, Chloe literally was the walking dead.

Psalm 139:8 (KJV)
If I ascend up into heaven, thou art there: if I make my bed in hell, behold, thou art there.

Titus 1:9 (KJV)

In hope of eternal life, which God, that cannot lie, promised before the world began

As the Word says, He is a man that shall not lie. As He promised Chloe, throughout her ordeal He would never leave nor forsake her. What an amazing journey when God says "No!" All things work for our good and for His Glory!

During the week to follow, the Holy Spirit would awaken Chloe three nights in a row. The first night, He spoke the word "Humility."

Chloe thought, *"Humility? What does that mean?"* The next day she looked up the meaning of the word. According to the dictionary, it means "the state of being humble" or "low."

Proverbs 11:2 (NIV)

When pride comes, then comes disgrace, but with humility comes wisdom.

Chloe had heard the word humble before, but never humility. *"Hmm,"* **she** **thought.** *"He's referring to coming before His presence praying on her hands and knees."*

The second night He said, "Lazarus."

"Lazarus?" she said. Finding the name in the Bible, she read about how much Jesus loved him and how He raised him from the dead.

Chloe noticed something interesting about the story of Lazarus. God, our heavenly Father brought him back to life. But when Lazarus came forth out of the tomb, he was still bound with grave clothes. He still had the stench of death on him.

God showed Chloe He was bringing her back to life. One would think when God called her to repentance, she would be completely delivered. Not just yet.

Mark 2:17 NIV

"On hearing this, Jesus said to them, 'It is not the healthy who need a doctor, but

the sick. I have not come to call the righteous, but sinners.'"

Chloe was alive again, but she was still bound in grave clothes. Chloe needed the grave clothes removed that were holding her back. You see, the old clothes (grave clothes) she had on were full of sin which was her sinful nature.

The third night, God said, "Be not conformed to this world."

Romans 12:2 (KJV)

And be not conformed to this world: but be ye transformed by the renewing of your mind, that ye may prove what is that good, and acceptable, and perfect, will of God.

What? Chloe had never heard of this scripture. However, the Spirit of the living God knew His Word. From that day on, God put a hunger in her like never before. A spiritual hunger. Chloe began humbling herself before the Lord. She would call upon the Lord, and hear Him say, "Come sup with Me," meaning, "come spend time with Me."

One day Chloe went into prayer. As she began to pray, her son would crawl over her. She wanted him to take a nap, because she was ready to hear from God. Chloe didn't let this stop her, but she pressed her way through and continued to pray. In a vision, God showed her the cross where Jesus was stretched out on the cross. There God stretched Chloe just like the Roman soldiers had stretched Jesus. God began stretching Chloe's arms. He kept stretching her. The experience left Chloe feeling the pain of being stretched just as she could only imagine the pain Jesus suffered on the cross. She knew He was doing a new thing within her.

Isaiah 43:19 (NKJV)

Behold, I will do a new thing, Now it shall spring forth; Shall you not know it? I will even make a road in the wilderness And rivers in the desert.

One night, Chloe and her son were sitting on the couch. They were the only ones home and fear arose within Chloe. Suddenly she opened her mouth screaming and crying, **"JESUS, I NEED YOU!"**

Immediately, the fear went away. The hedge of protection was placed back around Chloe.

She began devouring the Bible, she couldn't put this amazing book down. Story after story, God was opening Chloe's eyes to see the wonderful transformation in and around her.

Chloe finally read through the entire Bible. She was so proud of herself.

"I did it, Lord. What do I do now?"

The Lord said, "Read it again."

Okay...

Chloe read it again. She noticed scriptures in the bible she had missed. Chloe was so amazed. She especially loved Matthew, Luke, James and John. She loved the stories of Jesus shared by the apostles each had personally witnessed. **(Although Luke and**

James weren't eyewitnesses, she loved their books just the same)

REFLECTIONS

Strength

Barry experienced another job change. Once again, Chloe and Barry relocated. She didn't feel the sting of Barry's abuse, because she stayed in the presence of God.

Chloe read through the Bible again. Again, she was overjoyed! She asked the Lord, what's next?"

"Read it again," He said.

Oh, no! Not again! Chloe thought.

But she remained obedient. Chloe now read the Bible a third time. God was doing exactly what He said He would do through His Word., transforming her. Chloe was reading the Bible and listening to Christian radio.

One day, God drew Chloe to the radio and she started singing, "I know the plans, I have for You declares the Lord."

Chloe knew it was God's presence coming through the radio. He brought the scriptures alive through songs. Certainly by now, God would find something else for her to do.

Chloe asked, "Lord what do you want me to do next?"

He said, "Read it again, but this time, read it out loud."

Chloe responded, **"Oh Lord?!"**

But Chloe remembered some of the scripture.

Romans 10:17 (KJV)
Faith cometh by hearing and hearing by the word of God.

This time, Chloe did not follow God's instruction, because she read it aloud only sometimes. Reading the Bible out loud not only fed Chloe's faith, but also her spirit by speaking it out into the atmosphere.

REFLECTIONS

Ministering

Mark 11:24 (NKJV)
Therefore I say to you, whatever things you ask when you pray, believe that you receive them, and you will have them.

As much as God was changing Chloe, Barry continued to mentally abuse Chloe. But in the middle of the night, God would call Chloe to come sup (fellowship) with him. In the dark, Chloe would make her way to her prayer closet. There in the quiet, God would speak with her.

Eventually the abuse got so bad Chloe left Barry, but she would come back.

"Chloe…" Barry said. "I heard you praying all those nights you slipped away. I asked God, 'If only I could have half of what she has'."

Chloe didn't realize it, but God was beginning to break the chains off Barry, too. God was dealing with Barry in the still of the night. Barry wanted what Chloe had. The Lord reminded her about how God sanctifies the unbelieving husband through the believing wife.

I Corinthians 7:14 KJV
The unbelieving husband is sanctified by the wife, and the unbelieving wife is sanctified by the husband: else were your children unclean; but now are they holy.

God says no sometimes, just like every loving father does. When He chooses to say no, remember His goodness, remember His authority, remember His purpose, remember His promises.

Isaiah 55:8-9 KJV
For My thoughts are not your thoughts, neither are your ways, My ways, saith the Lord. For as the heavens are higher than the earth, so are My ways higher than

your ways and My thoughts than your thoughts.

Note to the Reader

Dear Reader,

REPENT, ask God into your heart and if you believe God raised Jesus from the dead on the third day, you will be saved. I am blessed to be alive and to share this story with you. Jesus loves you. He wants you to become His. Confess your sins and repent, turning from the things that held you bound. God will save you just like He saved me. *He just wants you to call on Him like you want Him...*

In Jesus' Holy name,
Amen

Epilogue/Prologue

Chloe was the victim of not only a breach of trust, but of abuse...so many times children are cast onto a road of acceptance of situations and experiences based on one act. These experiences and situations can be good or bad. Chloe is one such person...upon reflection, she realized the choices she made were not caused by the first imposing betrayal forced upon her. After all, we are all free moral agents and can choose which path to stay on...fortunately for her, with belief in God and a strong support system that started with her belief, she began to make different choices...next, let Chloe show you just how she chose to stay on her path while choosing different doors to open....

www.ingramcontent.com/pod-product-compliance
Lightning Source LLC
LaVergne TN
LVHW011911080426
835508LV00007BA/482